Compass Point
Phonics Readers

Where Animals Live

by Janelle Cherrington

Reading Consultant: Wiley Blevins, M.A.
Phonics/Early Reading Specialist

COMPASS POINT BOOKS
Minneapolis, Minnesota

Compass Point Books
3109 West 50th Street, #115
Minneapolis, MN 55410

Visit Compass Point Books on the Internet at *www.compasspointbooks.com*
or e-mail your request to *custserv@compasspointbooks.com*

Photographs ©: Cover: Corbis/W. Perry Conway, p. 1: Corbis/W. Perry Conway,
p. 6: PhotoDisc/PhotoLink/Scenics of America, p. 7: Bruce Coleman, Inc./David Ellis,
p. 8: Bruce Coleman, Inc./Erwin and Peggy Bauer, p. 9: Bruce Coleman, Inc./Erwin and
Peggy Bauer, p. 10: Corbis/Bob Rowan Progressive Images, p. 11: Corbis/Paul A. Souders,
p. 12: Corbis/Michael Pole

Editorial Development: Alice Dickstein, Alice Boynton
Photo Researcher: Wanda Winch
Design/Page Production: Silver Editions, Inc.

Library of Congress Cataloging-in-Publication Data
Cherrington, Janelle.
  Where animals live / by Janelle Cherrington.
     p. cm. — (Compass Point phonics readers)
  Summary: Shows the homes of an eagle, fox, bear, and bee in an
  easy-to-read text that incorporates phonics instruction and rebuses.
  Includes bibliographical references (p. 16) and index.
  ISBN 0-7565-0530-5 (hardcover : alk. paper)
  1. Animals—Habitations—Juvenile literature. 2. Reading—Phonetic
  method—Juvenile literature. [1. Animals—Habitations. 2. Rebuses. 3.
  Reading—Phonetic method.] I. Title. II. Series.
  QL756.C4835 2003
  591.56'4—dc21   2003006376

Table of Contents

Dear Parent or Caregiver,

Welcome to Compass Point Phonics Readers, books of information for young children. Each book concentrates on specific phonic sounds and words commonly found in beginning reading materials. Featuring eye-catching photographs, every book explores a single science or social studies concept that is sure to grab a child's interest.

So snuggle up with your child, and let's begin. Start by reading aloud the Mother Goose nursery rhyme on the next page. As you read, stress the words in dark type. These are the words that contain the phonic sounds featured in this book. After several readings, pause before the rhyming words, and let your child chime in.

Now let's read *Where Animals Live*. If your child is a beginning reader, have him or her first read it silently. Then ask your child to read it aloud. For children who are not yet reading, read the book aloud as you run your finger under the words. Ask your child to imitate, or "echo," what he or she has just heard.

Discussing the book's content with your child:
Explain to your child that the homes animals choose sometimes depend on the environment in which they live. For example, most birds build nests in trees. However, the Golden Eagle often lives in dry, rocky places where there aren't a lot of trees. Therefore, they build their nests in openings in the cliffs.

At the back of the book is a fun Tic-Tac-Toe game. Your child will take pride in demonstrating his or her mastery of the phonic sounds and the high-frequency words.

Enjoy Compass Point Phonics Readers and watch your child read and learn!

4

Higglety, Pigglety

Higglety, pigglety, my black **hen,**
She lays **eggs** for **gentlemen.**
Gentlemen come every day,
To see what my black **hen** doth lay.
Sometimes nine and sometimes **ten,**
Higglety, pigglety, my black **hen.**

Let's visit a cliff.
Who lives in it?

An eagle lives in a cliff.
It has eggs in its nest.

Let's visit a den.
Who lives in it?

A red fox lives in a den.
It has 1  pup .

Who lives in a box hive?
 Bees live in it.

A  can fly fast.
It can zig and zag and zap!

He can do his job.
A  bee can not zap him.

Word List

Short e
den
eggs
let's
nest
red

j
job

v
visit

x
box
fox

z
zag
zap
zig

High-Frequency
do
fly
he
where

Science
eagle
hive
live(s)

Tic-Tac-Toe

You will need:
- 5 game pieces for each player, such as 5 pennies and 5 checkers

Word Tic-Tac-Toe

nest	zap	visit
fox	red	eggs
where	he	job

14

How to Play

- **Word Tic-Tac-Toe** Players take turns reading aloud a word and then covering it with a game piece. The first player to cover 3 words in a row down, across, or on the diagonal wins.
- **Letter Tic-Tac-Toe** Players take turns naming a letter, saying a word that begins with that letter (such as *d, dog*), and covering the letter. The first player to cover 3 letters in a row down, across, or on the diagonal wins.

Letter Tic-Tac-Toe

d	w	j
c	r	b
v	y	k

Read More

Frost, Helen. *Bird Nests.* Mankato, Minn.: Pebble Books, 1999.

Galko, Francine. *Cave Animals.* Chicago, Ill.: Heinemann Library, 2002.

Longnecker, Theresa. *Who Grows Up in the Snow?: A Book About Snow Animals and Their Offspring.* Minneapolis, Minn.: Picture Window Books, 2003.

Schaefer, Lola M. *Honey Bees and Hives.* Mankato, Minn.: Pebble Books, 1999.

Index